Thirteen Acts of Love

A Guide to Loving Yourself More!

Jyotika

AuthorHouse™
1663 Liberty Drive, Suite 200
Bloomington, IN 47403
www.authorhouse.com
Phone: 1-800-839-8640

First published by AuthorHouse 6/4/2009

ISBN: 978-1-4389-2592-9 (sc)

Library of Congress Control Number: 2009901910

Printed in the United States of America
Bloomington, Indiana

This book is printed on acid-free paper.

Cover Photo: Gayle Goodrich

authorHOUSE®

For

*Todd Burke, my friend, my teacher, my **anam cara.***
He was a relentless mentor who never gave up on me
and whose passing gave selfless gifts that continue to inspire me.

♥

Contents

Preface

The more I embraced these Acts, the more countless opportunities appeared until I could see how I was creating my own pain.

For instance, an opportunity presented itself where it was clear that I was holding an expectation. This situation was supposed to end like **this,** not **that**. I was astonished to see that I was: 1) holding - a specific idea; holding anything stops the flow and creates resistance to what really wants to be happening now 2) expecting - the end result to be a specific pre-conceived idea 3) assuming - that this was going to end up in a certain way, not realizing that it could be different.

In this one experience my vibration was not aligned with many of the Acts. My reaction reeked of holding a position and defending myself which are major hints to look within. Then I saw how "assumption," "should," "past," "future," "expectation," "judgment," "surrender," "present" and "resistance" were all playing themselves out in this one experience. The Acts are very much a part of each other. They are one. They are inter-related; one feeds the other.

Seeing my self in this situation was difficult and uncomfortable at first. I kept looking and I could not see. Then one day the blissful AHA moment surfaced. It was so clear. Right there and then it was time to take responsibility. Surrendering to any possibility was a clear choice for it really wasn't mine to decide. I had to be willing to let go, to not have any expectations.

I was never more ready. I let it go, went to the other person involved, apologized and said, "I respect your choice. I will support whatever you decide." A feeling of calm and lightness of heart prevailed. I can say with a certain authority that I was walking on air.

The Acts will help you know, what you don't know, you don't know. It takes a little more courage and a determination to love your self more. Once you are there, it is not about courage and determination; it is about Being in your natural love state. It is meeting your true self again for the first time.

♥ Jyotika

Introduction

It started on a hike in the woods bordering Lake George, New York. I was visiting my dear friend Nancy Norman for a few days during my "Buddha Drive." (Now that is another story.) The first morning of my visit Nancy, her sister Shirley and I were "called" to hike through the woods to a vista overlooking the magnificent lake. This calling was enhanced by a bright sunny mid-spring day. We were drawn to nature to be nourished by the heat of the sun, the breath of the tall pines and the blue sky dotted with soft clouds reflecting in the lake and something unknown was to reveal itself.

We drove to the trail head, parked the car and started our adventure through the woods. We were not even a quarter mile into the trail when I heard a sound that was more familiar to me in the desert than in this tall pine forest of the stunning Adirondacks. It was the rattle of a snake very nearby. Not twenty yards ahead of us at the trail's edge were two beautiful rattle snakes, black with tan markings. They were fully engaged in a ritual dance. I was mesmerized by the sight. We quietly sat on a rock observing without disturbing the beauty of nature. The lovers were oblivious to us. Nancy had a camera with her and as unobtrusively as possible took a few shots, to capture this magical moment.

I remember the snakes' length at approximately five to six feet long. Their girth was the biggest I ever saw on a rattler. The ritual dance went on for a long time and yet there was no time. Presence dominated. They danced with the end of their bodies suspended at least three feet into the air pointing to the heavens. The music of their rattles and it's under song permeated their surroundings as they sensually wrapped and unwrapped and wrapped their bodies around each other again and again.

They were thoroughly engaged when we arrived and continued for what must have been an hour or more until suddenly they started to move in opposite directions of each other. Then they paused and began to ess their bodies followed by a backward motion toward each other once again. As we watched in quiet reverence, they touched lifting their rattles twelve to eighteen inches into the air, then he gently inserted into her for the briefest moment. They were complete. They went their separate ways. What a gift to be blessed with witnessing a rare and beautiful act of nature: rattlesnakes copulating.

That very night the **Thirteen Acts of Love** was born mysteriously and gloriously. I was abruptly awakened in the middle of the night. My eyes popped open to see the digital clock brightly shining at 2:22am. I bolted into an upright position and somehow knew to grab my journal. I simply held the pen to paper and allowed the words to come through. This recurred three nights in a row. The second night, once again at exactly 2:22am my eyes popped open and the download of information continued. The third night was different as the clock read 2:34am. This was my signal that the beautiful download process was coming to a close.

On the fourth morning sitting on the front porch which overlooked Lake George, a cup of tea in hand, I read through the previous nights' writings. The morning sun warmed me as I absorbed the words recorded in my journal. It became obvious to me that this was not only for me, but for all of us, for you and me who seek living with a peaceful heart.

Native American animal "medicine" holds the belief that snake "medicine" is very powerful. The influence of snake medicine is transformation, the shedding of the old to give birth to the new. Give birth to a new you by simply loving your self more. Allow the **Thirteen Acts of Love** to be a "tool" on your journey toward inner peace.

You will find the **Thirteen Acts of Love** familiar. You have heard each of them before. They are here for you to embrace as an instrument in your dance to love your self more, to embody as a way of life, to live life with a peaceful heart. The way they came through is very poetic in nature. Peruse the words slowly, feel them. Notice how they show up in your life. Remember that wherever your attention goes your energy flows and **that** is what you will get more of. It is the universal Law of Attraction[1]. Take your time, as the snakes did. Read one act per day and reflect on that Act throughout the day. Don't just read the words, realize them. Feel the power of their unconditional love. Embrace their wisdom. Let them fill you from the inside. As you fill with love and live from this connection to your inner being, everything that touches your field will be affected by this love as we were when we stood in the sensual field witnessing the snakes' love dance.

1 *Law of Attraction by Esther and Jerry Hicks*

Inner peace births world peace. . .
That is how important you are.

♥

Photo: Gayle Goodrich

Act One

Minimize Using the Words "should" and "supposed to"

Most often the words
should and supposed to
imply someone else's rule
imposed upon you
by a faceless norm.
Notice when **you** use these words.

PAUSE

Free of self-judgment
rephrase the sentence
without the words
should and **supposed to**.

Observe
how you feel.
Has the energy changed
from heavy to light?

Love your self more
by empowering your self
through your own conscious choices,
not someone else's rule.

As Osho said, "Should stinks of slavery."[2]

♥

2 *Autobiography of a Spiritually Incorrect Mystic by Osho.*

Photo: Joan Gregorio

Act Two

Unleash Judgments

Most importantly
release self-judgment.

There is no one
no where
who will judge you
more harshly
than you judge your self.

Love your self more
by releasing
all forms of judgment, comparison,
competition and pre-conceived ideas.

Let go of judging others.

Release comparison.
Allow everything and
everyone
to stand on their own.

Release competition.
Be your whole,
beautiful, powerful, self!

Unleash preconceived ideas.
See the naked truth
before you
and within you.

Don't judge
the judgment.
Simply notice, for:

Judgment s e p a r a t e s.

Love unifies.

♥

Photo: Gayle Goodrich

Act Three

Unshackle Expectations

Expectation breeds disappointment.

Focusing on the proposed expectation
causes you to miss
the magic of the moment
and what really
may want to be happening
here and now.

Hold your intention with soft edges.

Take one
fully explored step at a time.

Each step
determines the next step.

Be ready to take
a detour of discovery
in every instant.

There is never an end
only the magic
of every moment
of the Journey.

The mind gives imperfect information.

(continues)

Holding tight
to a specific idea
often creates
disillusionment
disappointment
discontentment.

The root of expectation is in the future.

Release the shackles
of your pre-conceived ideas.

Enjoy your life's journey.

♥

Photo: Gayle Goodrich

Act Four

Release the Past

Be grateful
for it has brought you
to this moment.

Realize
there is nothing you can do
to change the past;
it simply **is**.

All of your experiences thus far,
have contributed to your depth of character,
your strength
and your beauty.

Let the past go.

Carrying it with you
veils the now.

Love your Self more.

♥

Act Five

Let Go of the Future

It is not here yet.

Anything can happen
between
here and there.
Living in the future
causes you to miss
the Now.

Holding on to the future
creates suffering.
Therefore, you never really live
. . . you simply strive.

For the future never arrives.

♥

Photo: Gayle Goodrich

Photo: Irit Prize

16

Act Six

The Magic of Presence!

Experience the Now
without bringing any baggage,
pre-conceived ideas or attachments.

When you bring any form of
"the way you think it should be"
based on your past conditioning
to the NOW,
you veil the magic of **presence**.

Are you dragging the past with you?
Are you clouding the truth of the present moment?

The Now is pure,
a clean slate,
open and available
for the magic of
each unfolding moment.

It simply IS
without judgment,
expectation,
form,
supposed to's or
pre-conceived ideas.

Bring your whole self to every moment.

In the present moment
there is no time.

Merge with
the magic of presence.

♥

<u>Act Seven</u>

Return to Your Body

Yoga
is a wonder-filled tool.

Step onto your mat
for an hour and a half of
loving your self more.

Use meditative movement
to get back in touch
with you.

Unite
the body and mind.

Be
with what
IS.

Remember by forgetting.

Revitalize.

Dance with your Self.

Become whole once again.

♥

Photo: Irit Prize

Act Eight

Release Resistance!

Resistance opposes the flow
of what IS.

There is an undercurrent of **caution** in resisting.

Negative thought is resistance[3].

Life is flowing along and suddenly
something is in your path that you resist.

Why would you resist the flow,
create a **no**,
a challenge,
contract or
exercise caution?

Fear!

Fear is rooted
in the past
or the future.

Fear of the unknown is unfounded.

3 *Money, and the Law of Attraction by Esther and Jerry Hicks*

Notice when you resist.

Open your heart.
All it takes is a little more courage.

Embrace the adventure of the moment.

Release resistance
and allow
what **is**.

♥

Photo: Gayle Goodrich

Photo: Gayle Goodrich

Act Nine

Surrender

to the naked truth
of who you are.

ALL else
is imposed by
something
other than you.

Surrender,
Allow and
Accept.

Be with what is.

Get out of your own way.

Love more.

♥

Act Ten

Real Responsibility

Learn what is yours
to be responsible for
and what is not.

For instance,
parents often take on more responsibility
than what is theirs to take on,
thereby robbing the children
of their own experiences.

Accepting what is yours
and allowing others to accept what is theirs
raises humanity's vibration.

It just takes a little more courage,
a little more love
to own your mis-takes.
See them as opportunities.
Thus a stronger sense of self emerges without ego.

It is not all yours to do.
It **is** your duty to know when it is yours
and when it is not.

When it is yours, step up to the plate,
find the pearl in the experience
and focus on that pearl.

Don't accept more than what is truly yours,
We often do this to feed our sense of lack.
Don't evade responsibility either.
We often do this for lack of courage.

Take real responsibility
and know it is merged with intelligence.

♥

Photo: Irit Prize

Act Eleven

The Powerful Naked Word

The naked word
has the power
to release layers
of what is **not**
and reveal deeper truth.

Choose each word
with awareness.

Ask yourself:
Do my words harmonize with what I feel?
Do my words clearly communicate my intention?
Are my words flavored with manipulative energy to achieve an end?
Is what I am about to say an improvement on silence?

Ask the other:
To repeat back what they heard you say.
If it is not exactly what you intended to communicate,
maintain responsibility and
ask if you may again articulate
with more clarity
to say that which you wish to say.

Photo: Gayle Goodrich

The naked word
lends itself to
"short and sweet."

By short, it is meant to
remove any layers.
Say what you want succinctly.
Use less words!

Remove the "clothing" from your words
to reveal the core truth.
Naked words speak directly
portraying pure intent
eliminating misinterpretation.

By "sweet" it is meant
to allow your words
to stand in their nakedness
without emotion,
manipulation,
need or control
which may be buried
in the sub-conscious
Beneath
what you don't know
you don't know.

(continues)

27

By consciously choosing your words
you may also reveal
your deeper truth
to your self.

Naked words eliminate
idle chatter,
superficial noise
and gossip.

Create space
for the truth
to reveal itself.

Whether speaking or listening
allow quiet moments
between the words.

Get out of the way
with ease,
unattached to any outcome.

Effortlessly allow
what is meant to unfold.

DO NOT DRIVE IT
...RIDE IT!

♥

Act Twelve

Assume Nothing

Assume nothing
at no time.

Do not assume
someone else knows
who you are or
what you are
committed to.

Maintain responsibility.
Communicate.

Do not assume
you know
what the other
is thinking, doing or committed to.

Love more.
Listen more.

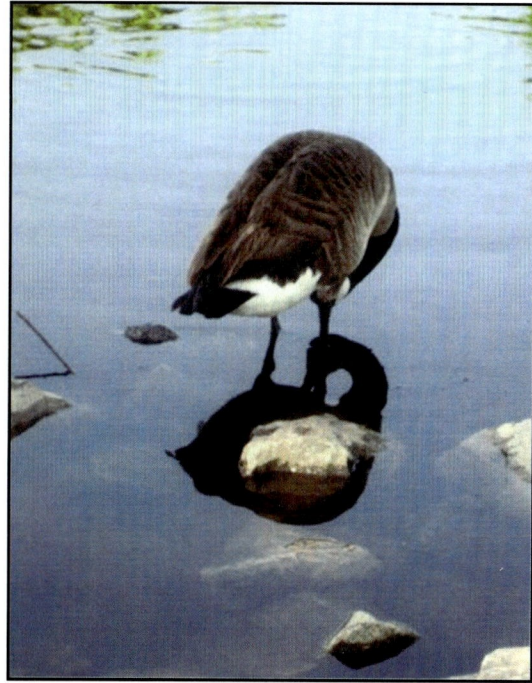

Do not **do** someone else's thinking for them.
nor answer for someone else
nor finish their sentences.

Do not interrupt!

Love more.
Fear less.

Create s p a c e.
Listen with your heart.

Releasing assumptions
clears the path
to Knowing.

♥

Act Thirteen

Quality Alone Time

Spend time alone **every** day.

Know the difference between
lonely and alone.

Create sacred time and
sacred space
every day and
in every way
to be with your Self.

In those alone moments
immerse your self in gratitude
for this moment,
for life,
its gifts,
and its opportunities.

Photo: Irit Prize

Forgive your self!
Forgive everyone!

Luxuriate in
grace, love, light,
health, harmony and abundance.
All that it takes is a little more courage,
a little more love.

Meet your self, again,
for the first time.

Become your own best friend.
Be the wind at your own back.

Know that you are never really alone.

Take your self out to dinner.

Celebrate you.

A s c e n D a n c e!

♥

So, Now What?

Now that you have read the Acts and felt them and absorbed them, it is time to integrate them into your life experience. Would you like to live with a peaceful heart, empowered and exuberant in each moment? Consciously bring the Acts into your life, relationships, work place and play, in every moment of your day. The Acts also serve as a foretaste to working clearly with the Law of Attraction.

Here are several suggestions for how to integrate the Acts into your life. Have fun with them.

♥ Read one Act per night. Preferably just before you go to sleep. Allow the vibration to work with you during the night. Reflect on that Act throughout your day.

♥ Choose your partner or a friend with whom to share the Acts. Take turns reading the Acts to each other. Read one act per meeting. Notice what it stirs in you and willingly share the questions or feelings that arise. Take your time. Allow what wants to unfold as you practice the Acts in real time. Create meaningful dialogue.

♥ Journal your experience that each Act has presented. Use this experience as if it is time with your best friend. Hold back nothing. Explore.

♥ Gather a few social-spiritual friends to form an "Acts Reading and Writing from the Heart" group. Explore one Act at a time and notice the depth of conversation/writing. Use the power of the naked word that leads to awareness.

♥ Notice how you feel as you embrace the Acts in all aspects of your life.

♥ Discover the wonder-filled world of yoga. Take a class.

♥ Participate in a Thirteen Acts retreat.

Acknowledgements

Todd Burke, relentlessly contributed to the depth of my continuous awakening during his life and in his passing. His eternal spirit continues to live in me and inspire me.
www.worldpeacetreaty.com

Nancy Norman who invited me to Tommy's home and shared the snake experience with me. Her literary mastery read every word of the Acts and contributed to its magic.
www.bellport.com/villageyoga

Tommy Linden whose house I was staying at when The Thirteen Acts of Love came through.

Gayle Goodrich, friend, follower of the path and amazing photographer. She captures the soul's light.
www.gaylegoodrich.com

Joan Gregorio, for her love and support through a lifetime of knowing each other. Her amazing photographs capture the truth of the moment and its perfection.

Irit Prize, dear friend and follower of the path; her pictures of nature and life as it happens, portray her connection to the moment with her artist's eye.

Jami Facchinello, my precious soul-sister. Karen Reider, sister-goddess. Mom and Dad, who brought me through. Joy Bibbins, my niece who helped with the computer challenges; and countless others whose love I share and am grateful for knowing.

Jyotika

by Karen Reider

Jyotika embodies a natural intelligence that can perceive the innermost needs and vibrations of people around her. This gift of perception can help guide you through what you believed, up to now, to be impossible conquests. Your words and thoughts are powerful catalysts for change. Jyotika's words are a catalyst for others' evolution. Beyond the lack you may have created, she can help those who have lost faith in themselves, retrieve their lost selves. She can guide you past your blocks and confusion to a place of freedom.

Jyotika will challenge you to raise your consciousness to the level of your noble soul, leaving aside ordinary indulgences so you may enter the royal road of your destined path. Remember the reason you walk in this world and help to create a world picture of love and peace. Begin the only way possible; remembering the grace and beauty of who you truly are. Inner peace births world peace that is how important you are! Step unwaveringly toward your own awakening and enjoy the journey.

Jyotika, often called a "mystical midwife," breathes life into those who have lost belief in themselves. Jyotika leads a free and healthy life with profound courage to walk her talk and share what has worked for her on a physical and spiritual basis. She embodies a unified lifestyle that she truly lives. She is ordained as an Ascendance Priestess, certified as a Kripalu Yoga teacher and other healing modalities. She intuits based on your focus and what you are ready for. Jyotika's loving presence, ability to hold safe, sacred space, her coaching talents, "tools of awareness," and more guide you into "The Art of Truly Living" your deeper truth.

Photo: Gayle Goodrich

Jyotika lives in Sedona, Arizona and Dania Beach, Florida. She offers the AscenDance Passage, 13 Acts Retreats, lectures, workshops, spiritual lifestyle coaching and more. Her work is designed for the uniqueness of each group or individual. Her passion is to serve the highest good for the greatest number.

www.jyotika.org   www.radhasradiance.com   diva@jyotika.org

Pages For Your Thoughts and Inspirations

Act One

Minimize Using the Words "should" and "supposed to"

_____

_____

_____

_____

_____

_____

_____

_____

_____

_____

_____

_____

_____

_____

_____

_____

Act Two

Unleash Judgments

_____

_____

_____

_____

_____

_____

_____

_____

_____

_____

_____

_____

_____

_____

_____

_____

_____

Act Three

Unshackle Expectations

Act Four

Release the Past

_____

_____

_____

_____

_____

_____

_____

_____

_____

_____

_____

_____

_____

_____

_____

_____

_____

_____

Let Go of the Future

Act Six

The Magic of Presence!

Act Seven

Return to Your Body

Act Eight

Release Resistance!

Act Nine

Surrender

Act Ten

Real Responsibility

The Powerful Naked Word

Act Twelve

Assume Nothing

Act Thirteen

Quality Alone Time
